WORLD CULTURES

Bushmen of Southern Africa

GALADRIEL WATSON

MEDIA ENHANCED BOOKS
AV2 BY WEIGL™
ADDED VALUE • AUDIO VISUAL

AV² provides enriched content that supplements and complements this book. Weigl's AV² books strive to create inspired learning and engage young minds in a total learning experience.

Your AV² Media Enhanced books come alive with...

Audio
Listen to sections of the book read aloud.

Key Words
Study vocabulary, and complete a matching word activity.

Video
Watch informative video clips.

Quizzes
Test your knowledge.

Go to www.av2books.com, and enter this book's unique code.

Embedded Weblinks
Gain additional information for research.

Slide Show
View images and captions, and prepare a presentation.

BOOK CODE

N864120

AV² by Weigl brings you media enhanced books that support active learning.

Try This!
Complete activities and hands-on experiments.

... and much, much more!

Published by AV² by Weigl
350 5th Avenue, 59th Floor
New York, NY 10118
Website: www.av2books.com   www.weigl.com

Library of Congress Cataloging-in-Publication Data

Watson, Galadriel Findlay.
 Bushmen of southern Africa / Galadriel Watson.
     p. cm. -- (World cultures)
 Includes index.
 ISBN 978-1-61913-094-4 (hard cover : alk. paper) -- ISBN 978-1-61913-529-1 (soft cover : alk. paper)
 1. San (African people)--Juvenile literature. I. Title. II. Series: World cultures (AV2 by Weigl) III. Series: World cultures.
 DT1058.S36W38 2012
 305.896'1--dc23
                              2011051105

Printed in the United States of America in North Mankato, Minnesota
1 2 3 4 5 6 7 8 9 0 16 15 14 13 12

062012
WEP170512

Senior Editor Heather Kissock
Art Director Terry Paulhus

Photo Credits
Every reasonable effort has been made to trace ownership and to obtain permission to reprint copyright material. The publishers would be pleased to have any errors or omissions brought to their attention so that they may be corrected in subsequent printings.

Weigl acknowledges Getty Images, Alamy, and Corbis as primary photo suppliers for this title.

CONTENTS

Where in the World?

TANZANIA

ANGOLA

ZAMBIA

MOZAMBIQUE

ZIMBABWE

NAMIBIA

BOTSWANA

INDIAN
OCEAN

NAMIB
DESERT

KALAHARI
DESERT

ATLANTIC
OCEAN

SOUTH
AFRICA

N

W E

S

SCALE

0   500 Miles

0   500 Kilometers

LEGEND

Bushmen Distribution

ATLANTIC
OCEAN

AFRICA

INDIAN
OCEAN

ATLANTIC
OCEAN

Population: More than
1 billion
**Indigenous Population
(Bushmen):** About
100,000
Continent: Africa
Nations: Namibia, Botswana,
and Angola
Area of Africa: 11,677,239
square miles (30,244,049
square kilometers)

Some experts believe the Bushmen have lived in southern Africa for about 10,000 years. Others believe the Bushmen have lived in this area for as long as 40,000 years. Regardless of when they first arrived in southern Africa, the Bushmen lived during the time of the **Ice Age**. At this time, nearly one-third of the world was covered with ice.

The Bushmen once lived throughout southern and eastern Africa. Over time, European **settlers** and other African peoples forced them to an area where few others dared to live. This area is called the Kalahari Desert. Today, about 100,000 Bushmen live in and around the desert, primarily in the countries of Botswana, Namibia, and Angola.

Traditionally, the Bushmen lived as hunter-gatherers. This means they hunted animals for meat and gathered plants such as wild vegetables and fruit. However, over time, their traditional way of

The Bushmen are the oldest inhabitants of southern Africa. They have lived as hunter-gatherers in this area for thousands of years.

life has changed. For example, in the early 1900s, about 60 percent of the Bushmen lived as full-time hunter-gatherers. By 1976, less than 5 percent lived as hunter-gatherers. Other Bushmen worked as farm laborers or lived on government **settlements**, which offered financial support. Today, government **persecution** prevents many Bushmen from practicing their traditional ways.

The Bushmen do not look like other African peoples. Many Bushmen are lean and stand about five feet (1.5 meters) tall. They have sharp-featured faces, dark skin, and tightly coiled hair.

There are many Bushmen **bands**. Each band has a name, such as !Kung, !Xo, G/wi, or Kua. Each band may have different customs and practices as well.

Culture Cues

🦒 The Kalahari Desert covers more than 190,000 square miles (500,000 square kilometers), making this desert larger than the entire state of California, which is 185,869 square miles (411,469 square kilometers).

🦒 Summer temperatures in the Kalahari can reach up to 104° Fahrenheit (40° Celsius). In winter, night temperatures become cooler, dipping down to about 40˚F (4˚C).

🦒 Animals that call the Kalahari home include the hyena, antelope, lion, wildebeest, and many bird and reptile species.

🦒 Although the Kalahari does receive some rain, it is very difficult to find water. In some areas, there are seasonal streams and a few permanent springs. Many areas have no surface water. In these areas, there may be water buried deep beneath the sand.

Stories and Legends

Bushmen stories often illustrate how these people survive in their harsh environment. Some stories tell of how the Bushmen hunt or pay respect to the animals they kill. Other stories explain how to find food or water.

The Bushmen enjoy telling stories. As one of their most common forms of entertainment, storytelling can last for many hours. Bushmen storytellers describe hunts, events, and gatherings. Sometimes, they simply **gossip**. Full of drama, the storyteller may gesture broadly or imitate the sounds of birds and animals.

One popular type of story is *n≠wasi o n!osimasi*, or "stories of the old people." Bushmen elders most often tell stories to fellow elders. These stories recount the days of long ago, when gods walked upon Earth and animals were people.

Many of the stories the elders tell are about Bushmen gods. For example, !Kung band members believe in a Great God. This god has eight names. They also believe in a Lesser God, known as Kauha the trickster. Many stories tell about his adventures.

According to Bushmen legend, the aardvark developed from a human who was digging to escape his enemies. Aardvarks are found throughout many regions of Africa. They dig holes with their powerful claws to find termites, their favorite food.

Other stories explore themes such as how the Sun first appeared or how death came to the world. Some stories explain how animals developed from humans. For example, the aardvark, or ant bear, developed when a human tried to escape pursuers by digging underground. After a while, his hands turned into claws, better suited to digging, and he became an aardvark.

Some Bushmen believe that if the shadow of a certain bird species is cast on a child, the child may become ill. If this happens to a baby, the Bushmen perform a detailed ritual that they believe will help cure the child of the illness.

The Bushmen tell many stories about the ostrich, too. One story explains how the ostrich was once a **gemsbok** antelope. Another story describes how the wise ostrich outsmarted the powerful lion.

According to Bushmen legend, the ostrich was once a gemsbok antelope. After seeing a Bushmen walking on two legs, the ostrich burned his front legs in a fire.

THE STORY OF
The Tsodilo Hills

The Tsodilo Hills are in the Kalahari Desert. To the Bushmen, these hills are **sacred**. This is one Bushmen story about how the hills developed.

Many ages ago, there was a man with two wives. Unfortunately, he loved one wife more than the other, and this caused many problems. While fighting, the wife who was loved less got very angry with the husband and hit him hard upon his head. This caused a large wound. She then ran away into the desert.

The Great God saw this fight. He told the husband and his wives that since there was no peace among them he must turn them into stone. The husband became the largest hill, with the gash upon its face. The loved wife and her children became the group of hills in the center. The unloved wife became the smallest hill farther off in the distance.

The Bushmen once called all of eastern and southern Africa home. Today, they live only in and around the Kalahari Desert. There are many different reasons why the Bushmen moved to this area.

About 4,000 to 2,000 years ago, another group of people emerged in southern Africa. This group, called the Hottentots, was descended from the same ancestors as the Bushmen. The Hottentot culture was similar to Bushmen culture. The only difference between the two groups was that the

Hottentots raised cattle instead of hunting and gathering like the Bushmen. The cattle competed with the wild game for grass. This forced the game to move to a new location. The Bushmen followed the animals.

In AD 200, another group of cattle herders, known as Bantu-speaking Africans, entered Bushmen territory. As the Bantu-speaking population increased, they gained control over more land for farming and grazing. This forced the Bushmen to leave the area in search of wild game.

Timeline of the Bushmen

40,000–10,000 years ago There are early traces of the Bushmen living in Africa.

AD 200 Bantu-speaking Africans move south, also taking control over Bushmen territory.

4,000–2,000 years ago Hottentot cattle ranchers force the Bushmen to leave their territory.

1652 The Dutch first settle in Africa, at the Cape of Good Hope.

1700s Clashes between Europeans and the Bushmen escalate.

1774 One European raid upon the Bushmen leaves 503 Bushmen dead and 241 captured.

In the 1600s, European settlers arrived in the region. As the settlers explored inland, they invaded Bushmen territory. The settlers killed the wild game without the Bushmen's permission. Upset by the settlers' lack of respect for their culture and land, the Bushmen killed many Europeans.

With such anger between the two groups, the Bushmen needed to leave the area. The Europeans had stronger, more powerful weapons, such as guns. They went on **expeditions** to kill as many Bushmen as possible. They sold other Bushmen into **slavery**. By the end of the 1800s, there were so few Bushmen alive they could no longer fight for their land. The Bushmen retreated. The only land remaining for the Bushmen was the Kalahari Desert. The climate and terrain was so harsh in the Kalahari that no other group wanted to live there.

In 1650, the Bushmen population was larger than 300,000 people. By 1955, only about 50,000 Bushmen remained. Since then, the population has increased to about 100,000.

1800s The last Bushmen are pushed out of southernmost Africa.

1961 The Central Kalahari Game Reserve is established and offered as a place for the Bushmen to live in their traditional ways.

2006 The High Court in Botswana rules that the Bushmen have a right to live on their ancestral lands.

1986 The Government of Botswana starts a campaign to drive the Bushmen out of the Central Kalahari Game Reserve.

1955 The Bushmen population declines to about 50,000 people.

1992 The Bushmen hold the first-ever regional conference on Bushmen peoples. Here they speak about issues such as education, health, social services, and jobs.

Social Structures

The Bushmen population is divided into groups called bands. Made up of relatives and friends, a band comprises several families. Each band has a husband, one or more wives, and children. Bands have about 20 to 60 people. There is no band chief or leader, although skilled hunters or older men may have influence over certain matters.

Each band has a territory covering up to 400 square miles (1,040 sq. km). The territory is selected according to the availability of water sources, plants and animals to eat, and trees for shade, shelter, and wood. Within this territory, the band travels from place to place when either food or water runs low. People also move from band to band, either through marriage, as a visitor, or in search of items to trade.

Men and women have daily activities they must perform. Men hunt animals. Women gather plants. Men prepare animal skins, later made into items such as clothes. Women make ostrich eggshell beads. Both males and females have equal power within the family and band. Both have the right to voice their opinions. Sometimes, they help do each other's activities, too.

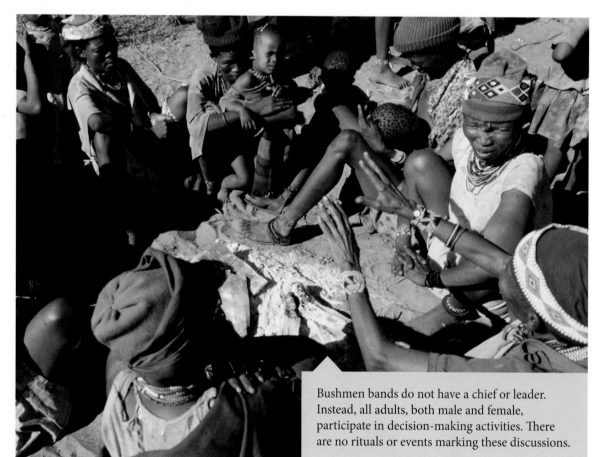

Bushmen bands do not have a chief or leader. Instead, all adults, both male and female, participate in decision-making activities. There are no rituals or events marking these discussions.

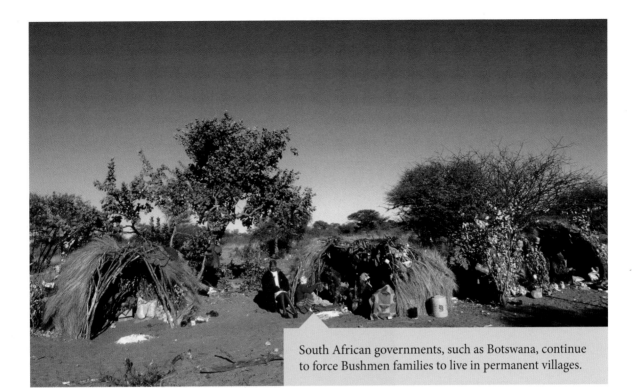

South African governments, such as Botswana, continue to force Bushmen families to live in permanent villages.

Children are not required to take part in daily chores. The children usually spend their time playing. Girls are usually about 14 years of age when they start helping to gather food. Boys are about the same age when they participate in their first serious hunt.

All members of a Bushmen community live together in open camps. Bushmen do not have much privacy. Other band members can hear any conversation that is louder than a quiet whisper.

The Bushmen use huts to store supplies. People only live inside the huts during extreme weather conditions. All band members share the open space and can roam freely throughout the campsite.

THE SEASONS

There are two distinct seasons in the Kalahari Desert. The rainy season extends from January to March. During this time, rain turns the desert green, and many plants grow. A Bushmen band can live in one area for several weeks before the local supplies are exhausted.

The dry season takes place between December and April. During this time, temperatures are colder and less plant food is available to the Bushmen. The band may split into individual households, each seeking food in a separate part of the band's territory.

Communication

The languages the Bushmen speak are called *Khoisan* languages. These languages are distinct from other languages because of their unique clicking sounds. Although there are many Bushmen languages, they can be divided into five general groups.

Since there is no English language equivalent to the Bushmen's clicking sounds, Khoisan words are written using letters and symbols from the English language. The following are a few of the most common words.

The letter *o/* sounds like "tsk, tsk." This sound is created by pulling the tongue away from behind the top teeth.

The letter *o=* makes a soft popping sound. This sound is made by pulling the tongue away from the ridge behind the top teeth.

The letter *o!* sounds like a sharp pop. Bushmen make this sound by pulling the tongue away from the roof of the mouth.

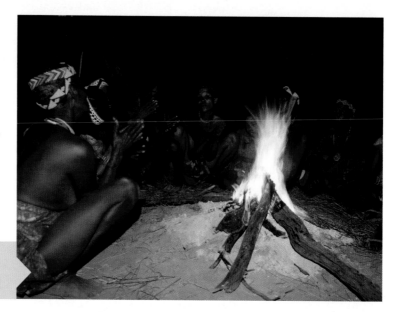

The Bushmen often tell stories while gathered around a campfire.

Name Game

In recent years, one of the Bushmen's biggest communication challenges has been deciding what to call themselves. Since there are so many Bushmen bands living in several different countries, many names have been used to refer to the Bushmen as a whole.

For example, in Zimbabwe, the Bushmen were called *Amasili* or *Batwa*. In Angola, they were sometimes referred to as *Kwankhala*. Dutch settlers used the name "Bushmen," but some Bushmen consider the term insulting. Others prefer the name "San," which is said to mean "bush dweller." However, others believe this name is also insulting. Some want to be called *N/oakwe*, or "red people."

The letter *o//* sounds like the English noise made to urge a horse to move. This sound is made by pulling the tongue away from the ridge behind the side teeth.

Most Bushmen languages did not have a written form until recently. For example, in 1989, **linguists** and other researchers helped the Ju/'hoan Bushmen create their own dictionary. This dictionary was published in 1994, and it is updated often. Today, there is also a Ju/'hoan/English dictionary, and Ju/'hoan children can read schoolbooks in their own language.

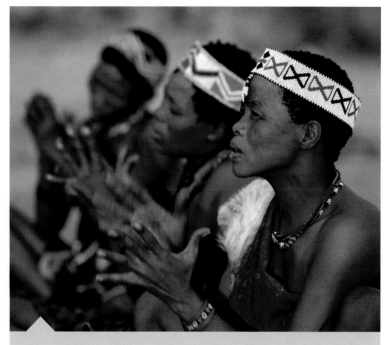

Dancing is an important form of communication. Women sit around a fire and clap to the rhythm of the songs. The men dance around the women.

The Bushmen have little use for mathematics. For example, when asked how many children a person has, the parent may not know the correct number. The Bushmen also do not have a system for keeping time, and they do not use the concept of years.

Throughout history, the Bushmen have used oral storytelling, song, and dance to pass their culture and traditions from one **generation** to another.

In Botswana, the Bushmen were most often called *Basarwa*, or "people of the south." In 1978, the Botswana government decided to call all rural people "Remote Area Dwellers."

To stop the confusion, in 1996, Namibian Bushmen representatives met and agreed to call themselves "San."

Law and Order

Bushmen obey a set of unspoken social laws. They share meat equally after a hunt. They show good manners by inviting guests to sit at their fire.

In general, the Bushmen avoid bad relations whenever possible. Although they sometimes take part in dangerous quarrels, the Bushmen usually obey a set of unspoken **social laws**.

For example, the fair sharing of meat after a hunt is very important. The person who owned the arrow that killed the animal divides the meat among the band. Sometimes, the arrow owner did not take part in the hunt. Still, this person divides the meat. The meat is always divided equally, and no one eats more than a modest share.

Bushmen women welcome visitors who are invited to sit at a fire. To welcome the visitor, the woman takes a sweet-smelling powder and sprinkles it over the visitor's head. This is just one of the many ways the Bushmen show good manners and keep order in their villages.

To receive food or a gift, Bushmen hold out both hands while the gift giver places the object in the receiver's hands. To hold out just one hand is considered grabbing and is impolite. In addition, strangers always lay down their weapons when first meeting new people.

Rather than become aggressive when angry, the Bushmen usually talk about their problems. To teach the youth to hold their tempers, the Bushmen may try to embarrass them by joking about their weaknesses.

When someone does not obey the rules, there are two main ways to bring the person back to order. First, the Bushmen may talk about the person. They may point out the poor behavior or hint at the problem. Second, the Bushmen may sing about the problem to show their disapproval.

Marriage is another important aspect of Bushmen life. Marriage is arranged by parents. Often, the first marriage is unhappy, and the couple divorces soon after the wedding. The man and woman then settle into new marriages. Some Bushmen marriages are **polygamous**.

Girls are often married as young as 7 years of age. However, these girls usually live with their parents until they reach **puberty**. Boys are usually about 14 years of age when they marry. Before they wed, boys must prove they can feed their families by performing their first successful hunt.

Bushmen boys and girls are equal in Bushmen culture. They begin sharing family and band responsibilities when they are about 14 years old. Boys begin hunting with the men. Girls help their mothers gather.

Celebrating Culture

Dancing is an important part of Bushmen life. The Bushmen dance after a birth, a marriage, sharing meat, when a girl reaches puberty, or after a boy's first kill in the hunt. Often, the Bushmen dance for fun. One of the most important reasons to dance is the *!kia* ceremony. This ceremony is performed by the !Kung.

The purpose of a !kia ceremony is to activate *n/um*. N/um is an energy that lies in the pit of the stomach. The Bushmen believe about one-half of Bushmen men and one-third of the women have n/um. They also believe n/um is **inherited**.

At the !kia ceremony, which usually lasts from dusk to dawn and takes place once or twice each week, the entire village gathers around a fire. The people at the center of the gathering sing and clap, while others dance around them. As a person dances, the n/um heats up and becomes a vapor. This vapor then rises up the person's spine to the skull.

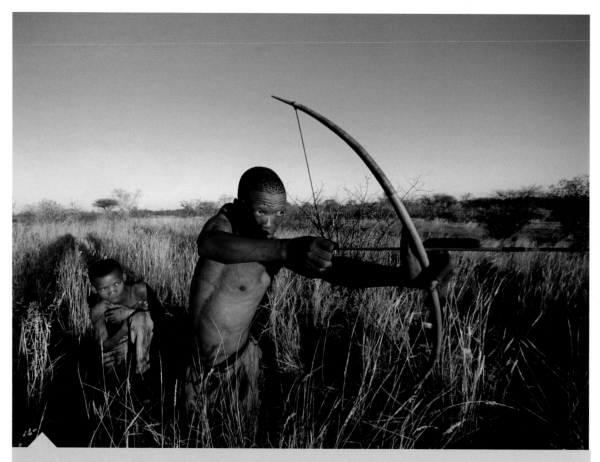

Often, the Bushmen use poison-tipped arrows to hunt. After a successful hunt, the Bushmen dance their healing dance. These dances often last throughout the night.

Bushmen children may encourage the n/um dance by singing and playing games around a fire. As the night progresses, children join their mothers in a circle around the fire while the men dance.

Once the n/um master is "in !kia," he or she can perform many tasks. The n/um master can help people with emotional concerns. This person can also see across long distances. The n/um master can use x-ray vision or walk on fire without becoming burned. A guardian watches over each n/um master to ensure there are no injuries.

One of the most important skills the n/um master has is the ability to heal. The Bushmen believe that a person becomes ill when dead ancestors choose to take the person to their realm. When in !kia, the n/um master struggles and argues with the ghosts. If the n/um master loses the battle, the sick person may die. If he wins, the sick person becomes well.

Having many n/um masters benefits the community, so the Bushmen encourage young people to develop their n/um. To do so, the "students" attend many !kia dances. While at these dances, n/um masters guide the students into accepting their n/um. However, the pain of the rising n/um, as well as the fear of not returning from the !kia state, stops many young people from realizing their potential.

Art and Culture

During rainy periods, the Bushmen store water in ostrich eggs. They bury the water-filled eggs in the ground for use in droughts.

Although the Bushmen do not record birthdays or anniversaries, they enjoy giving gifts for other occasions. They give gifts for **betrothals**, weddings, and a baby's first haircut. Sometimes, they give gifts even when they are not celebrating a special occasion.

Maintaining friendships is one of the main reasons the Bushmen exchange gifts. Nearly every item a person owns was given to him or her as a gift. These items may be given to someone else one day. The gifts are items the Bushmen use daily, such as a nicely shaped bowl or spoon carved of wood. The Bushmen take special care when making gifts because well-made items may be used for generations. The Bushmen do not spend much time decorating these items.

One art form the Bushmen practice is ostrich eggshell engraving. Hollow ostrich eggshells are used as containers, usually for carrying water. To engrave the shell, the artist scratches a design on its surface with a sharp knife. The artist then rubs the shell with **charcoal**, and the markings appear as black designs on the cream-colored shell.

Musical instruments are also an important part of Bushmen culture. The hunting bow is used as an instrument. Another instrument is the //gwashi. Traditionally, the Bushmen made this four-stringed instrument from a hollowed block of wood. They attached curved sticks and **sinew** strings to the wood. Today, the Bushmen make the //gwashi out of an empty food can.

The Bushmen also make other instruments. They make thumb pianos from flattened fencing wire and dance rattles from moth or butterfly **cocoons** that are filled with broken ostrich eggshells.

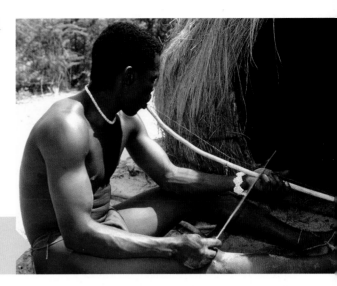

The Bushmen make musical instruments from a variety of items, including hunting bows.

Painting on Rocks

For thousands of years, the Bushmen practiced an art form called rock painting or **petroglyphs**. This art still exists today.

The earliest Bushmen paintings are about 6,000 years old. They are located throughout the southern African landscape. The pictures show people singing, running, or dancing at the !kia ceremony. They also show the local wildlife. Later paintings depict the European settlers' ships and wagons, and British soldiers wearing uniforms.

To make the pictures, the Bushmen may have used paintbrushes made of feathers, wildebeest hair, or hollowed bones. They used white clay, charcoal, and ground stone for color.

After the Europeans and other Africans forced the Bushmen to move to the Kalahari Desert, the Bushmen had few rocks to paint. The only rocks were in the Tsodilo Hills, which the Bushmen believe the Great God himself painted. Today, no Bushmen rock painters remain.

Dressing Up

After the Bushmen kill an antelope, the men stake the hide flat to dry. About one day later, they scrape the hide clean of fat using a sharp blade. If they plan to use the skin to make clothing, they scrape off the hair as well. Then, the men rub the juice of a **Crinum bulb** all over the hide. They may repeat this process many times. The Crinum bulb juice **tans** the hide and makes it flexible.

The Bushmen sew the hides into clothing with threads of sinew and needles of bone or metal. Most men wear a **loincloth**. The women wear front and back aprons. They hang leather slings, called *karosses,* from their shoulders. They use karosses to carry food, belongings, or infants. Today, the few Bushmen who still live in the traditional way may also wear tattered pieces of western clothing.

Ostrich eggshell beads are also important to the Bushmen. When an ostrich eggshell container breaks, the women gather the pieces, chop them into smaller circles, then punch holes into each piece. They string these beads onto sinew, creating long necklaces that reach to the belly button. They may also sew beads onto clothes, karosses, hunting bags, and headbands. Today, the Bushmen also use colorful glass or plastic beads, which they acquire through trade.

Men increase their attractiveness by shaving their heads, creating a pattern in their hair. This also helps keep their hair free of dirt and pests.

To make clothing, antelope hide is stretched out to dry. When it is ready, the soft hide is cut into different shapes and sewn together.

Bushmen sew beads onto clothes, karosses, hunting bags, and headbands. Today, the Bushmen sometimes sell these crafts to tourists.

BODY TALK

Both boys and girls are scarred for beauty and to mark certain rites of passage. For example, a boy is scarred on his face, arms, chest, and back after his first successful hunt. The scar is made by cutting the skin, then rubbing animal fat and plant **ash** into the cut. This ritual is performed on the right side of the boy's body if the animal was male and on the left side if the animal was female. The ritual is performed again after the boy kills an animal of the opposite gender. After receiving these scars, the boy is considered a man and is ready for marriage.

Girls are also scarred when they reach puberty. Scars are placed on the back of each of the girl's shoulders and in the middle of her chest. The Bushmen also celebrate the occasion by dancing, painting their faces like a gemsbok, and dressing in beaded clothing, necklaces, and headbands.

Food and Fun

Traditionally, the Bushmen are hunter-gatherers much like their ancient ancestors. Their diet consists mainly of plant matter, which is gathered by the women. The Bushmen eat about 150 types of plants, including wild vegetables such as **tubers**, fruits, and nuts. The //"xa, or *mongongo*, is an important food for the Bushmen. This fruit is widely available and has a nut of very high nutritional value.

Flying ants are a special treat for the Bushmen. During a two-day **infestation** of flying ants at the beginning of December, young women and children gather the insects. They collect thousands of the ants and roast them as food.

The men's job is to hunt. Antelope are very important, as well as other **herbivores**, such as wildebeest, kudu, and gemsbok. On average, a hunter kills about six large game animals every year.

Bushmen Diet

Wildebeest

Gemsbok

Tuber

Baobab Fruit

The Bushmen traditionally ate a varied diet of animal and plant foods. The plants they ate provided an essential source of water in the dry desert climate.

Leopard Tortoise

Warthog

Porcupine

Flying Ants

- Fruits and Vegetables
- Insects
- Red Meat
- Reptiles

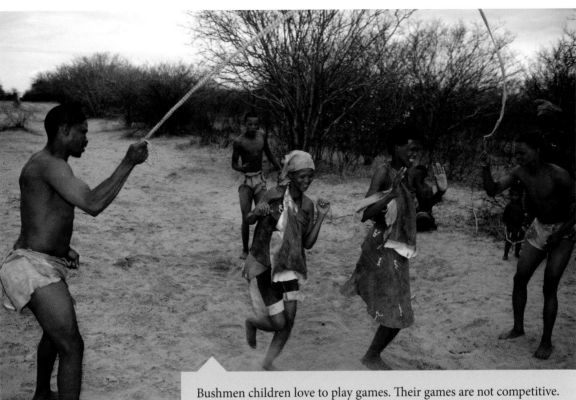

Bushmen children love to play games. Their games are not competitive.

They usually kill these animals with poisoned arrows, or they catch the animals in a **snare**. The Bushmen eat about 100 animal species. They hunt warthogs with dogs, and they use fire to drive African porcupines out of their burrows. The big leopard tortoise is easy to catch. Cooked in its shell, the tortoise can be a large enough meal to feed an entire family.

Today, few of the Bushmen rely on their traditional ways of life. Instead, they work for their food.

As for entertainment, the Bushmen enjoy talking, singing, dancing, and smoking tobacco. They also play games. Games are not competitive because each band has a limited number of children and few of the same age, gender, and skill level.

The Bushmen do not play team sports. Rather than competing against each other, children try to better themselves by watching others practice a sport.

One game the Bushmen play is called *zeni* or *ahna*. During this game, the Bushmen throw a feather that is tied to a weight, such as a pebble or nut. The feather and the weight are the zeni. The goal is to catch the zeni before it lands, then hook a stick onto it and throw it back into the air. This is repeated until the zeni hits the ground.

Children also play make-believe. They imitate the adults by playing house and hunting or gathering food. Sometimes, they make dolls out of unused tubers. They may throw a melon as a ball. They may also throw sticks and see how far the sticks bounce.

Great Ideas

Bushmen huts are made of branches, twigs, and grass. They look like upside-down birds' nests. In fact, the Bushmen do not live inside their huts. Instead, they use the huts as storage containers for their belongings. The land inside the circle of huts is used as an outdoor living area. During extreme rains or other weather conditions, the villagers may sleep inside the huts.

The Bushmen must be able to move their camp easily so they can search for food. As a result, they own few belongings. Some of these belongings are fire sticks.

To create fire, the Bushmen use their palms to quickly rub a piece of hardwood against a piece of softwood. The Bushmen place dry grass beneath the wood. The friction from rubbing the two pieces of wood together creates a fine dust that gathers on the dry grass. When there is enough of this dust, the Bushmen blow on the grass until it bursts into flames.

Bushmen start a fire by rubbing two pieces of wood together on dry grass.

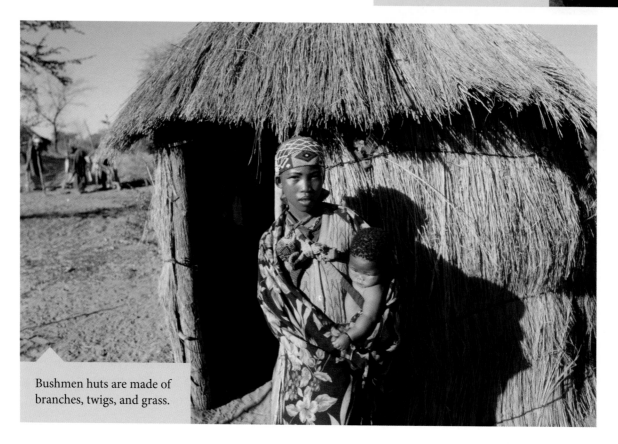

Bushmen huts are made of branches, twigs, and grass.

The Bushmen also own bows and arrows. The bow is made of wood that is bound with sinew for extra strength. The bowstring is made of two thin sinew strings that have been removed from the long back muscles of a large antelope. The Bushmen weave the sinew together to make a very strong rope.

A traditional Bushmen arrowhead is made of bone. Often, the Bushmen use an ostrich's shinbone to make arrowheads. Today, many arrowheads are made of metal. Using sinew strings, the Bushmen bind the arrowhead to a shaft of hollow reed, bone, and wood. The injury from these arrows is not strong enough to kill large animals. To kill their prey, the Bushmen coat arrowheads with a deadly poison. Most often, this poison is made from the **larvae** of the chrysomelid beetle. The poison kills the animal, but it will not kill the person who eats the animal's meat.

The Bushmen are successful hunters because they use their observation skills to track animals. While hunting, they seek clues to lead them to their prey. Bushmen hunters look at the direction hoofprints are pointing to determine which direction an animal is traveling. They look at the color of blood on the ground to learn when an animal was wounded and how long it will survive. They even consider the time of day and year when tracking an animal.

BEETLE POISON

The Bushmen use chrysomelid beetle poison to make their arrows more deadly. To obtain this poison, the Bushmen must first dig 1.6 to 3.3 feet (0.5 to 1 meter) underground to unearth cocoons. Each cocoon has one larva inside. There are three methods the Bushmen use to poison their arrows with the larvae. After removing the larva from the cocoon, the Bushmen squeeze its poison onto the arrowhead. They apply the poison from as many as 10 beetles to one arrow. Once the Bushmen have applied the poison, they dry the arrows over a fire. Another method the Bushmen use is to mix beetle larvae with plant juices and saliva. They then apply this mixture to the arrows. The third method is to dry the beetle larvae in the Sun. Once they are dried, the Bushmen grind the larvae into a powder. They mix the powder with plant juices and apply the mixture to the arrows. Over time, the beetle poison becomes less deadly. However, the poison remains strong enough to kill for up to one year.

At Issue

Few Bushmen today live in a traditional lifestyle of hunting and gathering.

Today, only a small number of Bushmen still live in the traditional way. Some of the Bushmen were forced off their land and placed in government settlements that are unsuitable for hunting and gathering. Others have lost their territories to cattle ranches or game reserves. Some of the Bushmen left their land to make **boreholes** in times of drought. They decided not to return to hunting and gathering.

Many of the Bushmen live on ranches, working for food, water, and shelter rather than money. Others raise their own crops and livestock. Some receive financial assistance from governments and international aid agencies. Others work as soldiers in government armies.

Many of the Bushmen live in poverty. Poor health is common, especially HIV/AIDS, as well as boredom, depression, alcoholism, and domestic violence. It is difficult for the Bushmen to receive medical attention, find jobs, or take advantage of business opportunities.

Tourists to the Kalahari sometimes see the Bushmen demonstrating their traditional way of life. Often, these Bushmen have been hired from the villages to wear their traditional clothing and show the tourists how to find water-filled tubers or catch an ostrich. At the end of the working day, these Bushmen remove the skins, slip on their modern clothing, and return to their villages.

The Central Kalahari Game Reserve

The Central Kalahari Game Reserve was formed by the Botswana government in 1961. The reserve land was established to allow the Bushmen to continue their traditional hunting-gathering lifestyle. The reserve was closed to the public, and about 1,000 Bushmen began living on the land.

In 1986, the government of Botswana decided to remove the Bushmen from the reserve. Many people believe this was to protect the interests of the diamond mines in the area. In 1997, 2002, and 2005, almost all the Bushmen were forced into settlements outside the reserve. In 2002, the government destroyed the reserve's only borehole and banned hunting-gathering there.

In 2006, the Bushmen went to court and won the right to return to their ancestral lands and pursue their hunting-gathering way of life. However, despite this ruling, the government refused them access to water. In 2011, the Botswana High Court ruled against the government and granted the Bushmen rights to water on the reserve.

Into the Future

Returning to the traditional way of life is not an option for most Bushmen. Instead, they are working to make a living in today's technological society.

Most Bushmen children attend school. Some schools teach these children in the Khoisan languages. However, many children must travel far from home to reach their schools. Often, few jobs await them when they graduate from school. Some of the Bushmen own small businesses. Others work in tourism.

Many of the Bushmen want land of their own. Until recently, the only band to have recognized land rights was the =Khomani of South Africa.

To improve their status, the Bushmen are actively involved in politics. For example, since Botswana gained **independence** from Great Britain in 1966, many of the Bushmen vote during elections. In some cases, the Bushmen must walk great distances to reach the election polls. They may face harsh treatment when they arrive at the polls. Still, many participate in these elections.

The first conference on the Bushmen peoples was held in 1992. At this meeting, Bushmen representatives gathered to talk about subjects such as education, health, jobs, and land. The governments of Botswana and Namibia also attended and pledged their commitment to help the Bushmen.

In recent years, however, the government of Botswana has been accused of denying basic rights to the Bushmen. A general election was held in Botswana in 2009. It was alleged that more than 400 Bushmen living within the Central Kalahari Game Reserve were denied the right to vote. In 2008, the U.S. Department of State noted that the Bushmen "lacked adequate political representation."

Many projects, funded by religious groups, individuals, or, in some cases, the government, are helping the Bushmen support themselves. One such group, the Kalahari Peoples Fund, offers local-language educational programs and curriculum, as well as financial assistance for initiatives such as job training, **handicraft** grants, and even soccer team uniforms.

Roy Sesana is a Bushmen leader who helped establish the legal right of the Bushmen to live on their ancestral lands.

Role-play Debate

When people debate a topic, two sides take a different viewpoint about one idea. Each side presents logical arguments to support its views. In a role-play debate, participants act out the roles of the key people or groups involved with the different viewpoints. Role-playing can build communication skills and help people understand how others may think and feel. Usually, each person or team is given a set amount of time to present its case. The participants take turns stating their arguments until the time set aside for the debate is up.

THE ISSUE

In 1997, 2002, and 2005, the Bushmen were pushed out of their homeland in the Central Kalahari Game Reserve. The government of Botswana destroyed their homes. The Bushmen were refused access to water. Many people believe the government did this to pursue diamond mining on Bushmen lands. In 2006 and 2011, the Bushmen won court decisions giving them the right to live in the Kalahari Game Reserve. However, development by the mining companies may endanger their way of life. The mining companies will build roads, fences, and permanent buildings.

THE QUESTION

Should the government restrict mining and development on certain lands in the Central Kalahari Game Reserve to preserve them for the Bushmen?

THE SIDES

NO

Government: The mines will provide employment for local people. The wealth from the mines will help our economy.

YES

Bushmen: The courts have upheld our right to live on our ancestral lands. Mining development may endanger our hunting-gathering way of life. The only people who will gain from the mines will be the mine owners and government officials.

Ready, Set, Go

Form two teams to debate the issue, and decide whether your team will play the role of the government or the role of the Bushmen. Each team should use this book and other research to develop solid arguments for its side and to understand how the issue affects each group. At the end of the role-play debate, discuss how you feel after hearing both points of view.

World Cultures Quiz!

1 About how many years do experts believe that the Bushmen have lived in southern Africa?

2 In what African countries do most Bushmen live?

3 What is the name for Bushmen artwork that has been preserved for thousands of years?

4 Why did the Bushmen move into the Kalahari Desert?

5 When do traditional Bushmen live inside huts?

6 What is the name for the languages the Bushmen speak?

7 In 1996, what name did the Namibian Bushmen decide to call themselves?

8 How do Bushmen divide the meat after a hunt?

9 How did the Bushmen carry water?

10 What decision did the Botswana courts make in 2006 that favored the Bushmen?

BOTSWANA let the Bushmen **live**
BOTSWANA DIAMONDS
BUSHMAN DESPAIR
THE BUSHMEN AREN'T FOREVER

ANSWER KEY
1. 10,000 to 40,000 years 2. Namibia, Botswana, and Angola 3. rock art or petroglyphs 4. because they were attacked and enslaved by European settlers 5. only during extreme weather 6. Khoisan languages 7. San 8. It is divided equally among people in the band. 9. in an ostrich eggshell 10. the right to live on their ancestral lands

Key Words

ash a powdery substance left behind when something is burned

bands groups of people who are related to each other in some way

betrothals when people make a promise to marry other people

boreholes deep holes drilled to release groundwater

charcoal a black substance produced when wood is burned

cocoons the silky protective coverings for insect larvae

Crinum bulb the bulb of a plant with strap-shaped leaves and flowers that grows in warm regions

expeditions journeys taken by people who have a specific plan

gemsbok a type of large antelope

generation people who are born at about the same time and have many things in common

gossip chatty conversation about rumors or facts

handicraft crafts made by hand

herbivores animals that eat plants

Ice Age a cold period when ice sheets covered much of Earth

independence to gain freedom from the control of another country

infestation when a large number of unwanted creatures are found in one place

inherited received from a relative or friend

larvae the wingless, worm-shaped forms of certain young insects

linguists people who study languages

loincloth a cloth that covers the hips

persecution when a group of people is treated cruelly

petroglyphs rock paintings

polygamous having more than one husband or wife

puberty the stage of life when a child becomes an adult

sacred worthy of respect

settlements areas set aside by a government to house a certain group of people

settlers people who come to live in a new place

sinew the tissue that attaches muscle to bone; also called a tendon

slavery being forced to work for someone

snare a trap used to catch small animals

social laws unwritten rules that guide how people behave

tans makes an animal hide into leather

tubers the fleshy, swollen part of underground roots or stems, for example, a potato

Log on to www.av2books.com

AV² by Weigl brings you media enhanced books that support active learning. Go to www.av2books.com, and enter the special code found on page 2 of this book. You will gain access to enriched and enhanced content that supplements and complements this book. Content includes video, audio, weblinks, quizzes, a slide show, and activities.

Audio
Listen to sections of the book read aloud.

Video
Watch informative video clips.

Embedded Weblinks
Gain additional information for research.

Try This!
Complete activities and hands-on experiments.

WHAT'S ONLINE?

Try This!	Embedded Weblinks	Video	EXTRA FEATURES
Map the area in which the Bushmen of southern Africa live.	Learn more about the Bushmen of southern Africa.	Watch a video of the Bushmen of southern Africa dancing.	**Audio** Listen to sections of the book read aloud.
Write a biography about a well-known person from the Bushmen of southern Africa.	Read about the history of the Bushmen of southern Africa.	See how the Bushmen of southern Africa live today.	**Key Words** Study vocabulary, and complete a matching word activity.
Create a timeline showing the history of the Bushmen of southern Africa.	View the arts and crafts of the Bushmen of southern Africa.		**Slide Show** View images and captions, and prepare a presentation.
Draw a chart to show the foods the Bushmen of southern Africa eat.			**Quizzes** Test your knowledge.
Test your knowledge of the Bushmen of southern Africa.			

AV² was built to bridge the gap between print and digital. We encourage you to tell us what you like and what you want to see in the future.

Sign up to be an AV² Ambassador at www.av2books.com/ambassador.